AUTISM
Alphabet
coloring
BOOK

I0459526

This Book Belongs to

_____

Autisum acceptance

Like others I deserve acceptance and appreciation, we should all be accepted for who we are.

Brave

When I overcome challenges and pursue my interest that makes me super brave !

Creativity

Creativity helps me express my feelings understand the world and have fun !

Doctor

My doctor makes sure I stay healthy and helps me reach my milestones.

EMotions

My emotions happen inside my body and shows on my face and movements.

Friends

Friends make me feel good.
I learn new things, and
we have lots of fun together.

Gestures

Gestures are like language!
It can help me communicate
when words are hard to come by.

Healthy

Eating healthy helps my mind and body work well so I can learn, play, and do the things I love .

Idenity

My Identity isn't only my superpower autism, but also my unique interest and strengths.

Jump

**Jumping can help me feel better
its a special way
to play and regulate my body.**

Kindness

Kindness is about treating others with respect and consideration.

Learn

I learn differently from others because my brain is unique and different.

Movement

I might do movements like flapping my hands, rocking, or spinning. It's a way for me to feel excited or calm.

Nonverble

I can't communicate with words , but that dosnt mean I can't communicate at all. I can use gestures and expressions.

Overstimulated

Too many experiences, sensations ,or activities can make me overstimulated.

Patience

Patience is important. I may process information differently and need time to adapt to situations.

Questions

I ask questions to seek information. It helps me better understand the world around me.

Routine

My Routine helps me feel safe and secure.
Its predictable events
that happen every day.

Strengths

My strengths are unique.
Such as strong attention to details,
Creativity, and problem solving.

Thrive

I thrive when I have a routine and supportive loving people around me that acknowledge my strengths.

Unique

Being unique is great .Your special qualities makes the world interesting.

Vigorous

Every day I wake up I try my best to be vigorous!

Wonderful

Every unique piece about me makes me wonderful!

X-factor

My X-factor is that special spark that makes me amazing at something.

You

You are amazing in so many different ways!

Zappy

Sometimes I can be zappy, energetic and fast!

Be creative draw a picture !

www.ingramcontent.com/pod-product-compliance
Lightning Source LLC
Chambersburg PA
CBHW080128150626
46550CB00017B/2834

9 7 8 1 9 6 4 9 6 3 8 2 2